EXTREME WINTER
SPORTS ZONE

SNOWBOARD SUPERPIPE

Darice Bailer

Ł Lerner Publications Company • Minneapolis

Lerner Publications Company
A division of Lerner Publishing Group, Inc.
241 First Avenue North
Minneapolis, MN 55401 U.S.A.

Website address: www.lernerbooks.com

Content Consultant: Nate Deschenes, senior editor *Snowboard Magazine*

With special thanks to Justine Spence, the U.S. Freeskiing press officer, for always being there to help. Thank you also to snowboarder Benji Farrow, Frank Wells of Snow Park Technologies, Tom Zikas, Shaun White, and Crystal Garrett.

Library of Congress Cataloging-in-Publication Data

Bailer, Darice.
    Snowboard superpipe / by Darice Bailer.
        pages   cm. — (Extreme winter sports zone)
    Includes index.
    ISBN 978–1–4677–0754–1 (lib. bdg. : alk. paper)
    ISBN 978–1–4677–1734–2 (eBook)
    1. Snowboarding—Juvenile literature. I. Title.
 GV857.S57B35 2014
 796.939—dc23   2012048753

Manufactured in the United States of America
1 – PP – 7/15/13

The images in this book are used with the permission of: © Ervin Monn/Shutterstock Images, 5; © Aaron Ontiveroz/The Denver Post/AP Images, 6; © Daniel Petty/AP Images, 7; © Nathan Billow/ Getty Images, 8; © Andrey Artykov/Alamy, 9; © Bongarts/Getty Images, 10–11; © Gabriel Acosta/ San Bernardino Sun/AP Images, 11; © Tom Hanson/AP Images, 12; © Vincent Curutchet/DPPI/Icon SMI, 13; © CanWest/Zuma Press/Icon SMI, 14, 29 (bottom); © Xinhua/Zuma Press/Icon SMI, 15; © Jean-Christophe Bott/AP Images, 16; © Aurelien Meunier/Icon SMI, 17, 28 (bottom); © Jean-Yves Ahern/Icon SMI, 18; © Christian Murdock/The Gazette/AP Images, 19; © Larry Pierce/Steamboat Ski Resort/AP Images, 20; © kubais/Shutterstock Images, 21; © Tony Donaldson/Icon SMI, 22–23, 29 (top); © Adam Neiland/iStockphoto, 24; © LORENVU/DPPI-SIPA/Icon SMI, 25; © ayazad/ Shutterstock Images, 26; © Marc Piscotty/Icon SMI, 27; © Kirster Soerboe/Scanpix Norway/AP Images, 28 (top).

Front cover: © iStockphoto/Thinkstock; backgrounds: © kcv/Shutterstock.com.

Main body text set in Folio Std Light 11/17.
Typeface provided by Adobe Systems.

TABLE OF CONTENTS

CHAPTER ONE

WHAT IS SNOWBOARD SUPERPIPE?

On January 29, 2012, something big was about to happen in the world of snowboard superpipe. It was a wintry evening in Aspen, Colorado. And it was the last night of ESPN's winter extreme sports competition, the Winter X Games.

The X Games are among the biggest extreme sports competitions in the world. Like the Olympic Games, winners can earn gold, silver, or bronze medals. Athletes also win prize money. Tonight was the finals for men's snowboard superpipe. The audience was ready to watch snowboarder Shaun White perform unbelievable tricks in the superpipe. The pipe was a U-shaped, snow-packed ditch with two 22-foot (6.7-meter) walls.

In January 2012, White was a 25-year-old snowboard and skateboard star. He had won the snowboard superpipe gold medal four years in a row at the Winter X Games. But some wondered if White would be able to ride as well tonight as he normally did. After all, White had sprained his ankle earlier in the week.

Pro Shaun White is one of the biggest stars of snowboard superpipe.

BOARD TALK

Catch air: get vertical height during a snowboard trick
Frontside: the side of the board where a snowboarder's toes are and the wall a snowboarder's toes are facing
Backside: the side of the board where a snowboarder's heels are and the wall a snowboarder's heels are facing

White began his run with a trick known as a backside air. First, he raced up the pipe with his back to the wall. Next, White soared 23 feet (7 m) above the pipe's rim into the night sky. He was 45 feet (14 m) above the ground. White sailed as high as the fourth floor of a building!

White landed safely. He raced up the other wall for his next trick. He did a frontside double cork 1080. White had invented this trick. And he was one of the few people who could land this tough move. In the trick, White did two flips while spinning around three times. One spin is a 360-degree turn. Three spins is a 1080-degree turn. While twisting, White grabbed the back of his board behind his boot heels. Then he uncorked, or landed on his feet.

THE SCORING

When riders compete at the Winter X Games, there are five judges. The judges watch for three things:
1. Amplitude, or how high the rider soars over the pipe
2. The technical difficulty of the tricks. The more rotations, the harder the trick.
3. Execution, or how well the rider performs in the air and controls the landings

The five judges then award a score from 1 to 100. The highest and lowest marks are thrown out. The judges average the middle three scores to decide who wins the gold, silver, and bronze medals.

White (center) earned the gold medal in the snowboard superpipe competition at the 2012 Winter X Games. Iouri Podladtchikov (left) won silver. And Ryo Aono (right) won bronze.

White's awesome run continued. On his next hit, or trick, he flew into the air. Then he flipped head over heels into a cab double cork 1080. *Cab* means White started the trick riding backward and finished facing forward.

On his sixth and final trick, White sped up the wall and rocketed skyward for a frontside double cork 1260. While spinning around three and a half times, White still managed to flip his body upside down twice! Then White landed as smoothly as if he'd never left the snow.

White's score was a perfect 100! No one had ever achieved a perfect score in snowboard superpipe at the Winter X Games before. White made snowboarding history again in 2013 when he took home the gold medal for the fifth straight year.

CHAPTER TWO

SUPERPIPE'S BEGINNINGS

*I*n New Jersey in 1963, a 12-year-old boy named Tom Sims wanted to skateboard in winter. Tom made a board out of plywood to ride on snowy streets. Tom covered the top of the plywood with carpet. The bottom was covered in aluminum. Tom called his invention a skiboard.

Inventing the Snowboard

Tom wasn't the only one looking for a way to take board sports to the snow. On Christmas morning in 1965, Sherman Poppen took two skis from his garage. He bolted them together so his daughters could ride down a snowy hill in their Michigan backyard. The girls had fun surfing the snow. Poppen's wife called the family's new toy a

The United States takes home more snowboarding medals than any country in the world. That may be because the sport began there.

The Holmenkollen Ski Museum in Oslo, Norway, features a display of vintage snowboards.

Snurfer. Soon a company called Brunswick began selling the Snurfer as a toy.

But the Snurfer was dangerous. Kids couldn't control it very well. There were no bindings for riders to strap their boots to the board. It often flew out from beneath riders. Sports enthusiast Jake Burton began thinking of ways he could fix the problem. He wanted to turn the toy into a real sport.

Burton got to work on his own board in 1977. He shaped the board a little wider so it could turn more easily. He also added bindings. Riders could strap their boots to the board to keep it beneath them. Burton attached metal edges to help control the board. These edges could cut into the snow and ice, helping the rider to steer.

Burton decided to call his creation a snowboard. The name stuck. He started a company called Burton Snowboards. And he began promoting the sport.

A Place to Ride

The sport became more and more popular. Eventually, a group of snowboarders decided to challenge one another to see who rode best. In 1982 snowboarders faced off in Vermont in the first national competition. It was called the National Snowboarding Championships. The event was a hit. Snowboarding was becoming famous.

Tom Sims was still involved in the sport. In 1983 he encouraged a California ski resort to build a pipe for the first snowboard half-pipe contest. It would be the first Snowboarding World Championship. The resort used a snowcat, a machine similar to a bulldozer, to pile up two rows of snow. Each row was about 4 feet (1.2 m) high. A U-shaped ditch was between the two rows. The ditch looked like the inside of half of a pipe. Now, instead of racing down hills, snowboarders were doing tricks off the top of this half-pipe.

The half-pipe changed the face of snowboarding.

When ESPN first began holding the Winter X Games in 1997, the network called the snowboarding competition Snowboard Half-Pipe. The walls were 11 feet 6 inches (3.5 m) high. The sport first appeared at the Olympic Games in 1998. Fans loved watching riders compete on the half-pipe. Soon pros were doing bigger and better tricks than ever before. It was time for a bigger pipe.

Kelly Clark soared her way to a gold medal on the 18-foot (5.5 m) half-pipe at the 2002 Olympic Games.

Half-Pipes Become Superpipes

Snowboarders were performing tricks with more spins, flips, and grabs. Pros needed higher walls to perform these tricks. In 2000 the Winter X Games half-pipe walls were built to be 15 feet (4.6 m) high. That year ESPN changed the name of the event to Snowboard SuperPipe.

By the 2002 Olympic Games in Salt Lake City, Utah, riders were using a half-pipe with 18-foot (5.5 m) walls. That year Americans Ross Powers, Danny Kass, and J. J. Thomas won gold, silver, and bronze medals, respectively, in the men's competition. American Kelly Clark won gold in the women's event. Doriane Vidal of France took silver. And Fabienne Reuteler of Switzerland won the bronze medal.

Seven years later, the pipe walls grew even taller! In 2009 the walls were sculpted to 22 feet (6.7 m) high. The walls of the pipe were supersized because the tricks were becoming even more daring and

spectacular. Riders needed the speed, the height, and the extra seconds in the air.

It was very dangerous performing tricks that fast and high. The pipe needed to be wider, making the walls less steep. The wider pipe meant more speed. The less steep walls meant that if pros fell, they didn't fall all the way to the pipe's bottom. The 22-foot (6.7 m) superpipe became the standard half-pipe size for all professional competitions.

HALF-PIPE OR SUPERPIPE?

A half-pipe can be any size. A superpipe is an extra-big half-pipe. Most superpipes are 22 feet (6.7 m) high. Some can be even bigger! But not all competitions changed their name as the Winter X Games did. Many professional events that take place on a superpipe still refer to the event as *half-pipe*. For example, the event is called Snowboard Half-Pipe at the Olympic Games. But the pipe is the same size as the superpipe at the Winter X Games.

CHAPTER THREE

RAD COMPETITIONS

Gretchen Bleiler competes on the superpipe at the 2010 Olympic Games in Vancouver, British Columbia.

Snowboard pro Elena Hight was just six years old when her father taught her to snowboard. Hight fell in love with the sport. She started competing two years later. Luckily for her, the United States of America Snowboard Association (USASA) runs contests across the country for riders of all ages. When Hight was 13, she qualified for the 2002 U.S. Grand Prix. It was her first professional event. There, she became the first woman ever to land a 900 (two and a half turns in the air) in competition.

ELENA HIGHT

Elena Hight may be only 5 feet (1.5 m) tall, but she's a big star in the pipe. Hight was just 16 when she made her first U.S. Olympic team. She was one of the youngest athletes at the 2006 Olympic Games in Turin, Italy, where she finished sixth in Snowboard Half-Pipe. Hight made the Olympic team again four years later and placed 10th in Snowboard Half-Pipe at the Winter Games in Vancouver, British Columbia, in 2010. In 2012 while practicing with the U.S. Snowboarding Half-Pipe Team, Hight landed a double backside alley-oop rodeo, or double cork. No woman had ever done that before! She went on to win the 2012 Burton U.S. Open.

The USASA helps young snowboarders improve. Every year the top riders can go to the USASA National Championships on Copper Mountain, Colorado, and show off their tricks.

If shredders (snowboarders) are good enough, they may be chosen for the U.S. Snowboarding Half-Pipe Team. Hight was on the U.S. Olympic team in 2006 and 2010. Six men and six women usually make up a pro team. Amateur snowboarders can be a part of amateur teams. Amateurs can move up to join the pros after winning national competitions.

Every four years, the Winter Olympic Games bring together top superpipe snowboarders from around the world. Chinese snowboarder Liu Jiayu earned fourth place at the 2010 Olympic Games.

Kevin Pearce had a shot at making it to the 2010 Olympic Games before he was injured during training in 2009.

STAYING SAFE

Snowboarding is fun. But it can also be very dangerous. Even pros take hard falls. In 2009 pro Kevin Pearce was practicing a trick when something went wrong. He slammed his head into the wall. Pearce hurt himself very badly. He had to stop competing. It is important for all riders to wear a helmet. Beginning riders should take snowboard lessons and stick to moves that an instructor feels are safe for them. No beginning rider should ever try to copy the pros.

Many U.S. snowboarders, such as Danny Davis, travel to Tignes, France, to compete on the superpipe at the European Winter X Games.

Snowboarding Pro

Professional teams practice for months. It takes a long time to master the difficult tricks snowboarders need to win medals at their events. Many pros and amateurs practice at the U.S. Ski and Snowboard Association training center in Park City, Utah. Here, riders can practice new tricks by landing safely on an air bag or in a foam pit.

Professional snowboarders travel all over the globe to compete. Their season begins in August and ends in March. A snowboarder might compete in six to eight major contests during the season. Between traveling for competitions and training, athletes can be away from home 10 or 11 months out of the year.

China's Xuetong Cai won the gold medal in the superpipe competition at the International Ski Federation Snowboard World Cup in 2011.

Competitions

The Winter X Games are some of snowboard superpipe's most exciting competitions. They occur twice a year, in Colorado and in France. Fans can watch the games in person or on television.

But the Winter X Games aren't the only big superpipe competition. Each year the International Ski Federation Snowboard World Cup brings together superpipe riders from around the world.

Burton Snowboards also holds the Burton Global Open Series each year. Snowboarders can compete at events such as the U.S. Open or European Open. At each event, the rider has the chance to earn points toward winning the whole series and a large cash prize.

The European Open is Europe's largest snowboard contest. It draws competitors from all over the world. At the European Open, junior snowboarders up to the age of 14 are invited to challenge the world's top pros. Winners can earn thousands of dollars in prize money.

The U.S. Revolution Tour is a three-stop series for young athletes. The Rev Tour, as it's called, has spots for junior riders ages 13 to 19, as well as older snowboarders. The juniors who score highest on the Rev Tour earn an invitation to compete at more major competitions. They're also invited to special camps on California's Mammoth Mountain. At the camp, snowboarders can learn more advanced tricks with the help of veteran riders. But the kinds of moves athletes show off at the Winter X Games and the Olympic Games are anything but easy.

A boy practices tricks into a foam pit at Woodward at Copper, a ski and snowboard camp in Colorado.

YOUR TURN, DUDE!

Hop on a snowboard, and new riders are bound to be hooked. Pros say snowboarding superpipe feels like flying!

Many resorts have half-pipes and some even have superpipes for snowboarders to ride. Most resorts have smaller half-pipes that are safer for beginning riders. To ride a half-pipe, a snowboarder has to know the basics. Signing up for a snowboard school, camp, or private lesson is the best way for rookie snowboarders to learn the sport. Many resorts have snowboard

Many ski resorts offer snowboard lessons to help new snowboarders learn the sport safely.

Snowboarding can be a dangerous sport. Make sure you've got all the right gear before hitting the pipe.

schools and camps for beginners. Some mountains make their own snow and have camps all year-round. Pros often teach at these camps during the summer.

Shredding with the Right Equipment

Snowboarders can choose from hundreds of boards and boots. It can be hard to know what to buy! Renting lets young riders try out different gear and decide what feels the most comfortable. All riders should also make sure they have the proper safety gear before hitting the pipe.

SHREDDERS GIVE BACK

Many snowboard stars use their fame to try to help others. Kelly Clark started the Kelly Clark Foundation. The charity encourages young people to snowboard by offering scholarships to kids who want to attend snowboard schools. Olympic champion Hannah Teter makes and sells maple syrup. She uses the money she earns to help dig freshwater wells and build new schools for children in Kenya. Every year pro shredder Louie Vito holds a snowboard contest for kids in his home state of Ohio. The contest is free. But kids have to donate an item for the local food pantry.

GEAR FOR SHREDDING

GOGGLES

Goggles protect a rider's eyes from the glare of the sun, the wind, and the snow. Snowboarding goggles should fit snugly and seal against the face.

JACKET, PANTS, AND GLOVES

Snowboarders need to stay warm and dry out in the snow. Riders should always dress for the weather, but they should be able to easily move around in their outerwear.

Pro shredder Keir Dillon wore the proper safety gear when he competed at the 2007 Winter X Games.

HELMET

A good helmet is extremely important in the pipe where athletes ride fast and high. The helmet should fit snugly and cushion the head. A helmet can help prevent serious injuries during falls. But it's important to ride carefully even when wearing a helmet.

PADS

Hip pads help to soften falls. These look like padded bike shorts and can be worn under pants. Knee pads and wrist guards also help protect snowboarders during rough landings.

BOOTS AND BINDINGS

Snowboard boots should fit comfortably and offer good ankle support. If boots are too loose, riders can't steer very well. If boots are too tight, they're going to hurt. Boots with soft padding inside are best for beginners.

A shredder drops into a half-pipe.

Get On Board

Entering a half-pipe is known as dropping in. Two lines of snowboarders may be waiting their turns at the pipe. When it's a rider's turn to enter the pipe, the rider raises a hand and says "Dropping!" or "Next!"

The best way to ride is using the warrior stance on the board. This stance involves bending the knees for balance. The arms are stretched out in front to stay balanced. Riders should relax their shoulders and look straight ahead to where they're going.

Pro Hannah Teter catches some air off the lip of the superpipe.

When it's time to ride, shredders should keep their knees bent and glide along the wall. Then they turn their boards toward the inside of the pipe and ride down the wall. Next, they can cut across the bottom of the pipe. Then they ride straight up the other side until they leave the lip and catch some air. After coming back into the pipe, a rider will be facing the other edge of the pipe.

GOOFY OR REGULAR?

Snowboarders have one of two stances. Regular stance is the most common. In regular, snowboarders ride with their left foot at the front of the snowboard. Goofy snowboarders ride with their right foot in front.

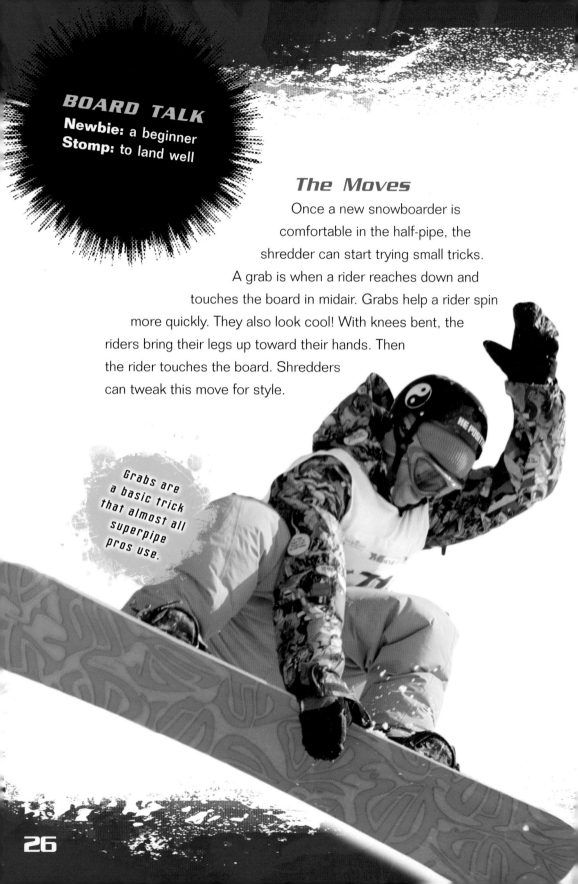

The Moves

Once a new snowboarder is comfortable in the half-pipe, the shredder can start trying small tricks. A grab is when a rider reaches down and touches the board in midair. Grabs help a rider spin more quickly. They also look cool! With knees bent, the riders bring their legs up toward their hands. Then the rider touches the board. Shredders can tweak this move for style.

Grabs are a basic trick that almost all superpipe pros use.

Once snowboarders have mastered different types of grabs, they can try adding spins to their grabs. With enough practice, they may work up to the kinds of tricks pros pull off in competitions. Half-pipe snowboarders are always trying to come up with the next big trick. Who knows—you might be the next Shaun White or Elena Hight!

SUPERPIPE
SUPERMEN AND SUPERWOMEN

BENJI FARROW

Benji Farrow grew up in Vermont, where his dad was a ski instructor. But Farrow fell in love with snowboarding. He gave the sport a try at the age of seven, and the rest is history. In 2012 Farrow won the bronze medal at the 2012 Burton U.S. Open and was named overall champion at the 2012 U.S. Revolution Tour. That same year, Farrow was added to the U.S Snowboarding Half-Pipe team. He would get the chance to compete for the United States in the 2014 Olympic Games.

LOUIE VITO

Louie Vito grew up in Ohio, where he competed in gymnastics through middle school. All that aerial training helped him flip through the air on a snowboard. Vito made the 2010 U.S. Olympic team and finished fifth in Snowboard Half-Pipe. The next year, he won the gold medal at the European Winter X Games in Tignes, France. Vito was the U.S. Grand Prix overall champ four years in a row, from 2008 to 2012.

KELLY CLARK

Kelly Clark started skiing in her home state of Vermont when she was two years old. When she was seven, her parents bought her a plastic snowboard. Clark was hooked. In 2002 she won the women's half-pipe gold medal at the Olympic Games. Clark has won every major event there is to win in snowboard superpipe. In 2011 Clark was the first woman to land a 1080 on a snowboard. In 2012 she earned her fourth gold medal for the superpipe competition at the Winter X Games. She won gold again in 2013.

HANNAH TETER

Hannah Teter grew up in Vermont with four older brothers. She started snowboarding in 1996 at the age of eight. When her brothers didn't want to ski with her one day, she took a snowboarding lesson instead. She is known for the creativity and height of her moves. Teter won the gold medal in superpipe at the 2004 Winter X Games. She won the gold medal at the 2006 Olympic Games in Turin and a silver medal at the 2010 Olympic Games in Vancouver. Teter has also won the Snowboard World Cup six times.

GLOSSARY

AIR

when a snowboarder leaves the ground

AMATEUR

someone who participates in an activity for fun without expectation of payment

DROP-IN

to ride downhill and into a pipe

GRAB

a trick where a rider reaches down and touches the board in midair

PROFESSIONAL

someone who participates in an activity as a job for payment

ROOKIE

someone who is new to a sport or activity

RUN

a set of tricks

SHRED

to snowboard

SUPERPIPE

a half-pipe with 22-foot (6.7 m) walls

SWITCH

to ride backward on a snowboard

FOR MORE INFORMATION

Further Reading

Bailer, Darice. *Snowboard Cross*. Minneapolis: Lerner Publications Company, 2014.

Doeden, Matt. *Shaun White*. Minneapolis: Lerner Publications Company, 2011.

Gustaitis, Joseph. *Snowboard*. New York: Crabtree Publishing, 2010.

Schwartz, Heather E. *Snowboarding*. Farmington Hills, MI: Lucent Books, 2011.

Websites

ESPN X Games
http://espn.go.com/action/blog/_/sport/xgames/
Check out the official X Games site to learn more about superpipe athletes, watch highlights from past Winter X Games, and find out when and where the next Winter X Games will be held.

Shaun White Biography
http://www.kidzworld.com/article/3706-shaun-white-biography
Learn more about superpipe legend Shaun White and how he began snowboarding.

U.S. Snowboarding
http://ussnowboarding.com/snowboarding
The U.S. Ski and Snowboard Association website has news about the team, pictures and profiles of its pro and rookie athletes, and information on how young boarders can start competing.

INDEX

About the Author

Darice Bailer has written many books for children. She won the Parents' Choice Gold Award for her first book, *Puffin's Homecoming*. She began her career as a sports reporter and is especially fond of writing about sports for kids. She lives in Connecticut with her husband.